Lessons from the Jericho Road

An Introduction to Authentic Pastoral Care

Darryl Claybon, D. Min.

Dante's Publishing • Atlanta, Georgia

Lessons from the Jericho Road
An Introduction to Authentic Pastoral Care
Copyright©2010
by Darryl Claybon

All Rights Reserved

No portion of this publication may be reproduced, stored in any electronic system, or transmitted in any form or by any means, electronic, mechanical, photocopy, recording, or otherwise, without permission from the author. Brief quotations may be used in literary reviews.

ISBN: 978-0-9827949-5-1
Library of Congress Control Number: 2010934969

"The scripture quotations contained herein are from the *New Revised Standard Version Bible* copyright 1989 by the Division of Christian Education of the National Council of the Churches of Christ in the U.S.A. Used by permission. All rights reserved."

Printed in the United States
Dante's Publishing
P.O. Box 39
Lovejoy, GA 30250-0039
www.dantespublishing.com
678-479-1216

For Information Contact:
Dr. Darryl Claybon
www.darrylclaybon.com
www.themacedoniaproject.com
404-213-6313

Cover design by Sally Kabukuru
Text design by Taneka Badie

DEDICATION

I dedicate this book to my loving parents, James and Dorothy Claybon. Their love, strength, courage, DNA, and guidance have proved to be invaluable and intrinsically interwoven into the fabric of my life. May they continue to rest in peace.

This book is also dedicated to Lee and Sharon, Elaine and John, Eunice and Johnny, Emma, Wilhelmina, James and Bernice, my cousins, uncles, aunts, nieces, nephews, and neighbors who have helped me to develop into the person I am today.

Most importantly, this book is dedicated to my students. You have impacted my life forever. And I am the better for it....

ACKNOWLEDGMENTS

To Bishop and Mrs. Marshall Gilmore, I will always be eternally grateful for their love, support, and kindness shown unto me. Their incredible ability to see in me, what I could not see in myself, will never go unappreciated and is judicially noted.

To Bishop and Dr. Thomas Brown, for their gifts of kindness to all of us, especially Angela, she loves you dearly.

To Bishop and Mrs. Hoyt, for their much needed love and support. To Bishop and Dr. Lakey, whose legacy will never be forgotten. To Bishop & Mrs. Carter, Elder Jane Thomas, Presiding Elders, Pastors and Members of the Sixth Episcopal District, thank you for your unconditional support. To the College of Bishops of the Christian Methodist Episcopal Church.

To Rev. Dr. J. A. and Mrs. Janice Milner and the Chapel of Christian Love: who provided incredible insight and illumination to my personal development and this project with patience and kindness. I was a stranger but you took me in....

To Mrs. Mignon Spencer (CEO) of Dante's Publishing who helped to ensure that I remained true to the task in a timely and orderly fashion. Thank you for understanding the writer in me, listening to my dreams and visions and making them a reality. May God continue to bless the work of your hands.

Thanks to Mrs. Susie Caswell, Mrs. Jane Jones, Yolanda, Timi, Karla, Melody, Dr. Bellinger, Dr. Jones, President R. Peters, Provost Edward P. Wimberly, and all of my colleagues at the ITC in Atlanta. Thanks to Charles "G Money" Garner for his coaching skills, Dr. J. "Pooh" Dawson for her skills in pastoral counseling, and Ms. C. Wilkes for timeless perseverance. Thanks to Rev. Vera Young, for her timely assistance and marketing skills.

My heartfelt **thanks** go to my friend and mentor, Dr. Michael I.N. Dash for his sincerity, faith, instruction, and wisdom given to me over the years. To the world you may be just one person, but sometimes to one person, you are the world.

I shall always be indebted to friends and family for their constant demonstration of love and support.

> Just let me live my life,
> let it be pleasing, Lord to Thee,
> and if I gain any praise, fortune, or fame,
> let it all go to Calvary.
>
> All that I am and ever hope to be,
> I owe it all to Thee.

To God be the glory, the honor, the praise!

Lastly, over the years, I have formed many relationships. All of you have been sources of inspiration to me. Thank you.

TABLE OF CONTENTS

Preface..vii

Introduction..ix

Chapter I: Who Needs Authentic Pastoral Care?..........................1

    Discussion Questions..9

    Case Study I..10

Chapter II: Who Can Administer Authentic Pastoral Care?..............15

    Discussion Questions..27

    Case Study II...28

Chapter III: What is Authentic Pastoral Care?...........................35

    Discussion Questions..41

    Case Study III..42

Chapter IV: What Happens After Authentic Pastoral Care?.............47

    Discussion Questions..59

    Case Study IV..60

Chapter V: "What then shall we say to these things...?" 65

Conclusion..73

Bibliography/References..74

Recommended Readings..75

PREFACE

The substance of these pages, in essentially the present form, was given as centering moments/meditations at The Interdenominational Theological Center during the course of studies in the Introduction to Pastoral Care Class. The purpose of this book is to provide tools to introduce "Pastoral Care" to the traditional and non-traditional adult learner. It is a series of centering moments (reflections from the scripture) using the story of the Good Samaritan as the narrative to explain authentic pastoral care.

The centering moments are the meditations used at the beginning of each class. The meditations are reflections derived from the scriptures to introduce the subject material of the lecture for the day. These centering moments are not exhaustive by any means. Nor suggest a comprehensive exegesis of the given text. But the intent and purpose is to first, allow the student to settle into the classroom. Usually when the students arrive for class, they have often experienced a very trying day. The students that take these courses are hardworking, family centered, faithful persons. Their day or week is full and their day planners do not have enough lines. Yet, they are taking the time to train themselves for the sake of building the kingdom of God. So the centering moments give them time to transition from boss, manager, supervisor, pastor, assistant pastor, minister, chaplain, caregiver, employee, mother, father, sister, brother, uncle, aunt, grandparent, etc. to student.

Secondly, the centering moments are designed to create, provoke, and stir up the gifts and imaginations of the student. The students say, "Tell us again teacher, what happened on the Jericho Road." And at that moment they too share their own experiences on the Jericho Road. The centering moments become more of a dialogue as opposed to a lecture. In this type of dialogue there are times the student becomes the teacher, and the teacher becomes the student. So please share your thoughts.

For more information about the classes offered by the Interdenominational Theological Center of Atlanta, GA, please contact:

> Mrs. Susie Caswell
> Program Manager
> 700 MLK Jr. Drive
> Atlanta, GA 30314
> 404.527.7766 or scaswell@itc.edu

INTRODUCTION

One might ask, "Why is the topic of authentic pastoral care relevant?" The answer becomes obvious to caregivers all over the world. First, as our world and economy has become an increasingly global environment over the past decades, so have our religious care needs. We have discovered that our destinies, no matter where we live, are intrinsically, interwoven together. With this understanding, many churches and denominations are engaged in global evangelism at this very moment, trying to reach the least, the less, and the lost.

Secondly, nearly all colleges and universities in the world are now offering at the core of their curriculum "World Religions" as a course. This is an opportunity for students to begin building a sensitive appreciation to the way others around the globe define and demonstrate their religious values and needs. Students that participate and compete successfully in a global economy must have some understanding of how religion plays a critical and crucial role in the way cultures around the world conduct business.

Thirdly, it is crystal clear, over the past decade, that ethics and integrity are essential for caregivers as well as corporations. As it relates to sweatshops and low pricing, many are willing to pay more if they know that human life is valued. We have learned that low prices do come with a price tag that many are unwilling to pay. We want to know how many labor laws have been overlooked to get this low price. We want to know if there is a child somewhere working ungodly hours without a lunch or water break. We want to know if companies operate under strong values and morals which encompass our belief systems. It is important to know how to minister to the needs of those in the boardroom as well as the needs of those in the sweat shops.

Therefore, as we discover that as different and diverse as our religious needs may be, those needs have a core essential quality. There is a need for us to understand the ways in which we can minister to each other as caregivers in a diverse and global environment. Because of the adverse, sometimes dark spiritual forces that operate in this world, there will be times when a spiritual helping hand is needed.

Therefore, "Pastoral Care" in its simplest terms can be defined as "the ways in which we minister to each other." Pastoral care is the ministry of care and counseling provided by pastors, chaplains and other religious leaders to members of their church, other congregations or persons within or outside a faith-based institution. This can range anywhere from home visitation to formal counseling provided by pastors who are licensed to offer counseling services. This is also frequently referred to as "spiritual care," which involves listening, supporting, encouraging and befriending.

Pastoral care is different from Pastoral Counseling. Under the auspices of American Association of Pastoral Counseling (AAPC), pastoral counseling adheres to rigorous standards of excellence, including education and clinical training, professional certification and licensure. Typical education for the AAPC-certified pastoral counselor consists of study that leads to:

- a bachelor's degree from an accredited college or university

- a three-year professional degree from a seminary
- a specialized masters or doctoral degree in the mental health field

A significant portion of this education is spent in clinical training. Post-graduate training involves completion of at least 1,375 hours of supervised clinical experience (that is, the counselor provides individual, group, marital and family therapy) and 250 hours of direct approved supervision of the therapist's work in both crisis and long-term situations. ("American", 2010, para 4).

Moreover, since our discussion is from a contemporary global perspective, "authentic pastoral care" means "specific pastoral or religious care given in a specific region of the world." Pastoral care in Opelika, Florida may look different from pastoral care provided in Northern Ireland, Spain, or North Africa. The type of care given depends on the culture and the resources available. Economies all over the world are somewhat precarious and are now facing many natural disasters. Disasters such as earthquakes that struck countries like Haiti and China as well as storms like Katrina and Ike, causing a steady supply of resources to not be available on any given day.

Although authentic pastoral care is general in scope, it is also generic and specific to the individual needing the care as the person giving the care. Authentic pastoral care is as simple as noticing that the single mom that lives next door may have a bad cold and may need some help with dinner and the dishes. It is as astute and elaborate as "Odyssey III," a multimillion dollar mission founded by Rev. Dr. J. A. Milner in Atlanta, Georgia, that provides services for the homeless and the mentally ill. It is how we minister to each other in a world that has allowed civility to become almost non-existent.

A Return to Civility

In terms of returning to civility, here is my theory: Many people in our culture have lost, misplaced, or never had home training in "table manners." There was an era when "dinner time" was the most important time of the day. It was a time carved out for families to gather for the evening meals and conversations, sharing an account of their days. It was there that we learned how to say "please" and "thank you, and not talk with our mouths full. We learned how to let others speak and not interrupt them as they spoke, no matter how burning our thoughts. At the dinner table we learned effective ways of communicating in verbal and nonverbal ways. At the dinner table, we learned to listen to each other. However, with families moving at sometimes breakneck speed, "dinner time" in some homes is almost nonexistent. Getting to soccer, cheerleading, baseball, football, track, band, violin, second jobs or tuba practice, while working crazy work hours sometimes means "dinner time" from the local drive-thru. Hence, it is hard to enforce table manners while driving, texting, and talking on a cell phone. Therefore, when people interact socially, their table manners are either lost or nonexistent in translation and in interpretation. Therefore, some people we meet in today's culture are not as civil as people once were.

The Narrative Perspective

"Genuine pastoral care, from a narrative perspective, involves the use of stories (personal, from the practice of ministry, and the Bible) by pastors to help individuals and familial groups to visualize how and where God is at work in their lives and are thereby able to receive healing and wholeness." (Wimberly, 1991 pg. 9) As we begin our studies, we agree with Dr. Wimberly, that the stories used by pastors are drawn from her/his personal life, practice in ministry, and stories from the Bible. Moreover, in terms of authentic pastoral care, we would add that ministering to another person is not limited to just pastors and ministers.

Christianity, Protestant Churches, Catholicism

Pastoral care usually involves shepherding the flock. This is a loving way of caring for people. In Protestant churches pastoral care, therefore, both encourages local congregations, and brings new parishioners into the church. This is not to say that the congregation is not to be involved in both activities, but that the pastor should be the initiator. (Wikipedia) In terms of Catholic theology, pastoral care for the sick and infirm is one of the most significant ways that members of the Body of Christ continue the ministry and mission of Jesus. Pastoral care is considered to be the responsibility of all members of the body. (Wikipedia) As we shall see in the following discussions that everyone can be involved in ministry.

Lessons from the Jericho Road

Using the story of the Good Samaritan on the Jericho Road, we shall explore four important lessons in contemporary authentic pastoral care. As we understand the Samaritan, he is not a priest or Levite (church officer), yet he is able to minister to a wounded stranger that is in need. We shall shape our discussions around the four questions as presented in the Good Samaritan story: First, who needs authentic pastoral care? Secondly, who can give authentic pastoral care? Thirdly, what is authentic pastoral care? And finally, what happens after authentic pastoral care?

We will begin our study with the first question: Who needs authentic pastoral care?

Lessons from the Jericho Road
An Introduction to Authentic Pastoral Care

CHAPTER I
Who Needs Authentic Pastoral Care?

Jesus replied, "A man was going down from Jerusalem to Jericho, and fell into the hands of robbers, who stripped him, beat him, and went away, leaving him half dead." (Luke 10:30, NRSV)

Jesus is responding to a question by a lawyer whose interest lies in the definition of the term "neighbor". Jesus begins this story by telling his listeners about a man who is embarking upon a journey. He is traveling down from Jerusalem to Jericho. This road that the man is traveling is called the "Jericho Road." The listeners of this parable are familiar with the Jericho Road. It is a well traveled road.

It is apparent that this man who is traveling down to Jericho had some significant business in Jerusalem and pressing business in Jericho. He is leaving the Holy City, Jerusalem, and traveling to Jericho, the Promised Land. A journey we all must make, physically and spiritually. Jericho, a deep and fertile hollow, is a distance of 19 miles northeast of Jerusalem. This rocky and desolate road was a notorious haunt of robbers, then, for ages after, and even today. Warren Wiersbe suggests, "The road from Jerusalem down to Jericho was indeed a dangerous one. Since the temple workers used it so regularly, you would think the Jews or Romans would have taken steps to make it safer. It is much easier to maintain a religious system than to improve the neighborhood." (Wierbe, 1989, p. 364) Martin Luther King, Jr., offered in one of his famous sermons, "It was a winding road with plenty of nooks and crannies. It is here thieves and robbers could easily hide in blind spots." We can all agree that the road of life is very similar to the Jericho Road.

As the man travels, he falls into the hands of thieves and robbers, who strip him, beat him, and go away leaving him half-dead. Through what appears to be no fault of his own, the man runs into this trouble. He "falls" into the hands of "thieves." (KJV) He appears to be minding his own business and yet trouble comes. He is leaving Jerusalem, no doubt after having conducted and completed some Temple business. Perhaps he was even making offerings and saying prayers in the Temple to the Most High God—yet on the way home, trouble finds him.

Again, the robbers and thieves strip him, beat him, and go away, leaving him half-dead. They take everything he has including the shirt on his back. The robbers pound, punch, and strike him in the face, on his head, and hammer his body mercilessly. Then, the robbers go away leaving him half-dead. Half-dead has to be an incredible state of being, ebbing and flowing, back and forth, vacillating between life and death. Depending on the next few moments, he could be closer to death than life. Half-dead suggests that the man is in a position in which he cannot help himself. The individuals that authentic pastoral caregivers seek to aid are "those who cannot help themselves." They are the people who need a break; they need a hand up and not a hand-out. They need a chance, an opportunity to get back on their feet so they may continue their journey from Jerusalem to Jericho. In a moment's time, the traveling man's life is changed forever. Like the millions that have lost their jobs during the last recession, their lives have been changed forever. It is indeed a paradox that people that used to give generously to soup kitchens and groceries lines, now stand in those same lines in need of soup and groceries for themselves.

Sobering Thoughts

There are a few things that are extremely sobering in the text so far. First, it appears that Jesus is saying/implying/conceding that there are some forces in this world which are beyond our control. These forces will strip, beat, and leave unsuspecting persons half-dead. In the story of the Good Samaritan, these forces are represented by thieves.

Secondly, these forces attack people randomly, not necessarily as the result of the choices they made. Not withstanding, we have freewill and responsibility. And from time to time, we all make some very bad decisions that have very bad consequences. However, we do not know enough about this man to suggest that he made other bad choices in his life. Jesus says he falls into the hands of thieves. I am hard pressed to believe that the millions of people who have lost their jobs during the recession of 2000, all made bad choices. It is written that *"the rain falls on the just and the unjust."* Not all of the people that are facing foreclosures made poor choices. When the biblical patriarch Job was faced with foreclosure he argued that *"the Lord giveth and the Lord taketh away, blessed be the name of the Lord."*(KJV) Job felt in his heart of hearts he had done all of the right things. This included making daily offerings for his children, just in case they had done some things that were not right and failed to ask for forgiveness. Yet trouble still comes. Job also asked, after being cross-examined by his wife, *"Shall we not receive good at the hand of God, and not receive evil?"* (KJV) Job is suggesting that this attack is not necessarily divine retribution or repercussion, but perhaps the sovereignty of God at work.

The forces that rob, strip, beat and leave a person half-dead challenge Old Testament theology and compel additional thinking. Psalms 37:25 reads: *"I have been young, and now am old, yet I have not seen the righteous forsaken or their children begging bread."* (NRSV) It appears that in this current economic climate, some of the children are begging for bread. However, we are only able to see the now, and not just necessarily the future. Therefore as for our duty toward those who now face adverse situations, such as foreclosure and unemployment, it is our duty to reassure and encourage them as the songwriter does who says: "I see your future, and you look better!"

Thirdly, this text, in my opinion, suggests that Jesus is not just necessarily in the "prevention business" but perhaps more in the healing, restoration and resurrection business. This man falls into the hands of robbers. He is stripped, beaten, and left half-dead. While the man is being stripped and beaten, there appears to be a lack of divine intervention in preventing the attack. We would like to believe that this man prayed for "traveling mercy" and yet trouble meets him on the road. We can extrapolate that the divine intervention occurs in the sense the traveling man is not killed or that help does arrive at some point. However, this attack is not prevented from happening. We all ask from time to time, "Why good things seem to happen to bad people and bad things seem to happen to good people?" Could this be one of those times... since we cannot make presumptions about the character of the wounded man?

Most of us, if not all, have prayed for Jesus to protect us from all hurt, harm, and danger. Yet, most of the time, when we are calling on Jesus, the damage is already done. There are times when we have prayed for Jesus to prevent things from happening. And in countless instances, Jesus has prevented disaster from occurring. Notwithstanding, let us continue to hear the whole story. For in the midst of this misfortune, perhaps we shall see the hand of God working on the behalf of this wounded man. While the wounded man has met with despair, he is in no wise forsaken. 2 Corinthians 4:7-9 states:

> "But we have this treasure in clay jars, so that it may be made clear that this extraordinary power belongs to God and does not come from us. We are afflicted in every way, but not crushed; perplexed, but not driven to despair; persecuted, but not forsaken; struck down, but not destroyed." (NRSV)

A Word about Jesus and Thieves

Jesus appears to have a systematic theology and an affinity for thieves. Jesus refers to them often: *"Lay not up for yourselves treasures upon earth, where moth and rust doth corrupt, and where **thieves** break through and steal."* (Matt. 6:19, KJV, emphasis added),

*"And said unto them, It is written, My house shall be called the house of prayer; but ye have made it a den of **thieves**."* (Matt. 21:13, KJV)

*"All that ever came before me are **thieves** and robbers: but the sheep did not hear them."* (John 10:8, KJV)

*"The **thief** cometh not, but for to steal, and to kill, and to destroy: I am come that they might have life, and that they might have [it] more abundantly."* (John 10:10, KJV)

Jesus refers to his behavior as that of a thief: *"And this know, that if the goodman of the house had known what hour the **thief** would come, he would have watched, and not have suffered his house to be broken through. Be ye therefore ready also: for the Son of man cometh at an hour when ye think not."* (Luke 12:39-40, KJV)

Jesus even dies between two thieves: *"Then were there two **thieves** crucified with him, one on the right hand, and another on the left."* (Matt. 27:30, KJV)

Moreover, the first to enter the kingdom of heaven as we understand it is a thief.

> *"And one of the malefactors which were hanged alongside Jesus railed on him, saying, 'If thou be Christ, save thyself and us.' But the other answering rebuked him, saying, 'Dost not thou fear God, seeing thou art in the same condemnation?' And we indeed justly for we receive the due reward of our deeds: but this man hath done nothing amiss. And he said unto Jesus, 'Lord, remember me when thou comest into thy kingdom.' And Jesus said unto him, 'Verily I say unto thee, today shalt thou be with me in paradise.' "* (Luke 23:39, KJV)

Predestination

I am often challenged by caregivers who believe that people are in the position they are in because of the choices that they made. I certainly believe in freewill and consequences. However, I believe that the traveling man on the Jericho Road would probably have made a different choice had he known what awaited him on that fateful day.

The battle with addiction has always been intriguing. It is amazing how some people can have youthful indiscretions and dealings with drugs, alcohol, and other substances (legal and illegal), and when ready, seemingly walk away and never look back. Unfortunately, it appears some people are **not** allowed to walk away at their discretion. Recovery can sometimes become a life-long battle. Are the ones that are able to walk away somehow smarter, or physically, mentally, or spiritually stronger?

At the end of Luke 10:30, the reader is left wondering what will happen to this man. It appears through no fault of his own; he has fallen and cannot get up. Jesus describes him as half-dead, or in other words "within inches of death." This truly must be as close to Hell on earth, as one can get. He has been robbed, beaten, stripped and left half-dead. The traveling man is in a position in which he cannot help himself. And in my humble opinion, he is the epitome of the kind of people that need authentic pastoral care: "People that are unable to help themselves!"

DISCUSSION QUESTIONS

1. Why do you believe there is no divine intervention as the traveling man is attacked?

2. Is it the traveling man's fault that he is attacked?

3. Can addiction be a part of a person's "destiny" or "predestination"?

4. Do you think God could have prevented the 9/11 attack? Why do you think God did not prevent the attack?

_____
_____
_____
_____
_____
_____
_____
_____
_____
_____
_____

CASE STUDY I

Setting: Sunday school teacher Rob has been told by one of his adult members (Joe), that he needs to talk. Joe says there are some things that are going on, and it's pretty bad.

However, a couple of weeks go by and Joe never makes an appointment. Finally Sunday school teacher Rob calls Joe and they set an appointment for the following Sunday.

During the Sunday morning class, Sunday school teacher Rob announces that he is not to be disturbed after class. "Cause I'm going to be talking with Joe" is the way he put it.
(Joe and Sunday school teacher Rob meet.)

S.S. Teacher Rob: How's it going?

Joe: Not too well….

S.S. Teacher Rob: Well when I was your age, it didn't go too well with me either. Those young girls just would not leave me alone. I was what you might call a ladies' man. I had "them lined up," know what I am saying….

Joe: Not really…I just want to tell you, that the reason I miss church sometimes is because I have been taking drugs and it is really affecting my work and personal life….

S.S. Teacher Rob: Well son, you know what the Bible says about drugs; if you keep taking them, you are going straight to hell. And you are going to burn in the lake of fire, with fire and brimstone. No sir, the Lord only loves a cheerful giver, and remember, He helped 'ole Gilligan get off the island...you got to put the drugs down boy....

Joe: Well I tried, but the drugs will not leave me alone.

S.S. Teacher Rob: See that's what's wrong with young people; you think you know everything. That's what I tell my son, but of course he doesn't listen to me, calls me the 'ole preacher man... but I raised that boy, and he does not listen, even with those big 'ole ears like a bunny rabbit.... Let's read this scripture and pray, and you are going be healed right here and now. I am going to lay hands on you, bring in the elders with that anointing oil and, you'll be fixed in no time.

S.S. Teacher Rob *(buzzes intercom to secretary)*: Send for the elders. We are going to anoint 'ole Joe!
Joe leaves before the elders arrive.

CASE STUDY QUESTIONS

1. What does the Sunday school teacher do correctly?

2. Is it a good thing to announce to the class personal information? Why or why not?

3. During the meeting, is the Sunday school teacher in the listening mode? Name three things that indicate that the teacher is not listening?

4. What three actions show us that Joe is trying to explain his situation?

5. Do you think the teacher is in over his head? What are some things the teacher can do to really help Joe?

_____
_____
_____
_____
_____
_____

YOUR THOUGHTS

CHAPTER II
Who Can Administer Authentic Pastoral Care?

Is it Just The Pastor's Job?

Now by chance a priest was going down that road; and when he saw him, he passed by on the other side. So likewise a Levite, when he came to the place and saw him, passed by on the other side. But a Samaritan while traveling came near him; and when he saw him, he was moved with pity. (Luke 10:31-33, NRSV)

At the end of verse 30, the reader is left wondering what will happen to this man. He has fallen into the hands of robbers and is within inches of death. He is unable to help himself. The story, up to this point, has been very unsettling; however in verse 30, it appears that the story is about to get back on track.

Now by chance, a priest is going down the same road. For those who ascribe to the theology of predestination, "by chance" is more than a notion. This is more than "by chance"; it has been orchestrated by the hand of the Almighty God. Though the story is truly troubling, "by chance" things are about to change. A priest sees him. At this juncture, we feel a sense of relief because the traveling man's calamity will now be relieved. As we understand the priest, the priest is one that has unlimited and direct access to the throne of grace as well as the power of prayer on his side. Surely the priest will call upon the power of God to intervene in this situation. Prayer will change things. The traveling man will recover and his injustice vindicated.

But there is another turn in the story—a thickening of the plot, if you will. Dr. Edward Wimberly offers four parts to the narrative: unfolding, linking, thickening, and twisting. God's plot unfolds one scene at a time; one cannot know the end of the story until the entire drama is completed. When one identifies with stories that have an eschatological plot (end of time) in Scripture, one is not only pointed toward God's unfolding story in the midst of life, we are also linked with the dynamic that undergirds the plot. (Wimberly, 1991, p. 14)The behavior of the priest and the Levite is called the thickening of the plot. Thickening refers to those events that intrude into God's un-folding story and seeks to change the direction of that story for the ill of all involved. (Wimberly, p. 15)

The priest sees him and passes by on the other side of the road. It is very easy to be critical of the priest. We feel that he should have stopped to help this man. Perhaps this is where Dr. R. L. White, pastor of Mt. Ephraim Baptist Church of Atlanta GA, would suggest the need for Soren Kierkegaard's Teleological Suspension of the Ethical. That no law or rule should be so narrow, that there cannot be at least one exception to the rule. However, before becoming too critical, we must show some compassion for this priest.

We are not able to understand what the priest's day must have been like. Perhaps, this was the priest's day to be on 24-hour call at the hospital, and he is simply trying to make it home. Perhaps the priest is wrestling with his own demons. Many scholars believe that the priest was being obedient to the law, and he did not want to defile himself in any way. Even today many priests, pastors, and caregivers have to make judgment calls. It is psychologically impossible to answer every phone call.

Many pastors are facing burnout today because they have

stopped too many times on the Jericho Road. They have missed too many soccer games, baseball games, football games, and cheerleading practices, trying to help others. Some pastors, ministers, and caregivers miss too many dinners, parades, picnics, and family/spouse times all because they stopped to help someone along the way.

One chaplain, who worked for Grady Hospital in Atlanta, recalled how he had been on-call over-night. There was a bad accident on the highway that involved a school bus full of high school students. The accident happened about 1:00 AM and the emergency room was packed until 9:45 the next morning. His shift ended at 6:00 AM, but there was no way he could leave. The chaplain said, "We were so busy tending to the needs of the children in the emergency room and the frantic parents on the phone that none of us even had a chance to get a rest break or any food to eat. Blood, screams, and prayers filled the night." As the chaplain is going home, he passes by an accident. One of the drivers appears to be seriously injured. He witnesses more blood and even more screams at yet another accident site. The chaplain said he thought about stopping, just maybe he could be of assistance. However, as he pulled over, and attempted to get out of his car, he realized he was just too weary. He said a prayer while sitting in the car, but he decided to let the paramedics handle this one. He went home.

Compassion Fatigue

In psychology we use the term "compassion fatigue." There is a gradual lessening of compassion over time and a gradual increasing level of cynicism, pessimism, and disdain. It happens when a caregiver is continuously involved in cases and start to distant themselves from the person being treated. The caregiver may say:

"Oh, here we go again!"

"I have heard your story before; you are going to tell me, it was not your fault."

"Why do you people let yourselves get into these situations?"

It also stands to reason that if pastors, ministers, or church leaders can suffer from compassion fatigue, they may also suffer from **compassion dementia** or even **compassion absentia**. Compassion dementia happens when one becomes so far removed from reality, or so heaven bound, that they forget when they have been in a state of helplessness. Compassion absentia is a more critical condition for it suggests that the caregiver has never experienced or received compassion, therefore, has no frame of reference, or may even lack the ability to extend compassion.

The Messiah Complex

In ministry, many suffer from what is known as the "Messiah Complex." The "Messiah Complex" is a state of mind in which the individual believes he/she is, or is destined to become a savior. These individuals feel that they have to help or save every single person they encounter as well as save the world. And they feel they have to do all of this while raising a family and maintaining a successful marriage. Oftentimes pastors, priests, and caregivers who suffer from this syndrome feel their calling is to change the world by specializing in the search and rescue business. In other words, they actually seek out people that need help and provide assistance, often at the caregiver's own peril.

However, in this story we believe Jesus is trying to make a point. The priest sees the wounded man and passes by on the other side. Also, the Levite, who represents the other church officers, sees the wounded man and passes by on the other side. And before we become too critical of the Levite, his day at the Temple may have been filled with overwhelming activities. He, too, may have been on call for the last 24 to 48 hours; and all he wants to do is get home.

We should be highly suspicious of church officers and members that are present every time the church door opens. Let's examine the week long schedule for an average church officer. There is Sunday worship service, which in some cases consist of two worship services. On Monday there is a Board Meeting. Tuesday night is Choir Rehearsal, Wednesday night is Bible study, and Couples' Class is on Thursday night. On Friday night, there is teen night or maybe camping or other activities. On Saturday there is a bake sale, clothes closet, and car wash. And less we forget the week long revivals, church anniversaries, Mother's Day, and Father's Day programs, there is always some activity going on at the church. And, most church officers work regular jobs and volunteer outside the church as well. I do understand Jesus' point fully in this story; however, I hope that we are not too critical of the Levite.

I propose that for some busy church members, it will be a sad day when getting to heaven, and seeing everyone else's family members, but none of their own. They have spent their entire lives tending to church related matters, and have missed tending to what really matters! After all, the family is our first ministry. According to the scriptures, Jesus stopped dying long enough to ensure that his earthly family affairs were in order. Heaven and earth were waiting on Jesus to die that salvation might begin. But, according to John 19:26-28,

> When Jesus saw his mother and the disciple whom he loved standing beside her, he said to his mother, "Woman, here is your son." Then he said to the disciple, "Here is your mother." And from that hour the disciple took her into his own home. After this, when Jesus knew that all was now finished....

(KJV) Only **after** Jesus tends to his own family affairs, does he continue with the plan of salvation.

Finally Help Arrives!

But a Samaritan while traveling came near him; and when he saw him, he was moved with pity. (Luke 10:31-33, NRSV) In verse 33, the listener can breathe a sigh of relief for help has finally arrived. This help is not the most likely person that the hearer would expect to respond to the travelling man. He is a Samaritan! In this particular time of history, Samaritans are despised by the Jews, yet it is a Samaritan that stops and offers help. When he sees the wounded man, he is moved with pity. He has compassion on him.

Who can administer authentic pastoral care? First, it is the person who is filled with compassion and pity. The person administering authentic pastoral care must have the capacity within him or herself to demonstrate compassion. The Samaritan does not think of the dangers lurking on the Jericho Road. The Samaritan is not consumed with his own world, schedule or agenda. His concern is not the threat of other robbers or the community in which he has stopped. Martin Luther King in his famous speech "I've Been to the Mountaintop" offers "His question is not what will happen to me, but what will happen to this man, if I do not stop and help him."

Secondly the person administering authentic pastoral care must be able to recognize or discern when a person has a genuine need. While at times it may be very obvious who is in need, there may be times when it is not so evident. Sunday morning Church services provide the greatest opportunity for many people to wear masks and attempt to hide their wounds and scars and camouflage their struggles. Sunday morning Church services are also when people in need are attempting to put their best foot forward and weather their ferocious storms. The people that come through the doors of the church are wounded in so many ways and on so many levels. They are simply looking for tools and techniques, perhaps even a word, that will turn the tide and shift the momentum of those brutal and violent storms in their life to more favorable conditions. Their plight may not be as obvious as those non-church goers, but it is just as detrimental and damaging.

Church Membership

Perhaps the day will come when the Church will recognize the need to offer more than one way to join the Church and what it means to be a member of a church. Today, if someone wants to join the Church, they have to wait until the worship hour. What happens if the person is hospitalized or immobilized, or in this case of the wounded man in our story, half-dead on the road to Jericho? Does this mean they have to wait until the Sunday worship service to become a member of the Church? And even then, there is a litany of steps the wounded soul must endure before they can be recognized as full-fledged members in some churches. Gone are the days when one could simply join the Church. As much as I understand the scrutiny that many churches put prospective members thru, I am grateful that on the day I decided to join the Church back in the summer of 1980, I was able to join that day. I did not have to wait until my background check cleared; the Church took me at my word. And no, my walk has not been perfect since that day. I have stumbled, even fallen at times, and I thank God no one decided to remove my name from the Church roll.

Personal Discernment

The authentic pastoral caregiver will be able to recognize a person in need best by understanding the moments in their own life when they have fallen among thieves. Authentic pastoral caregivers are acutely aware of the times when they have been beaten, stripped, robbed and left for dead. We do not have enough information to know whether the priest and Levite had any similar experiences. However, we do know that the Samaritan is moved with such compassion that he suspends his own journey to help this man in need. Perhaps the Samaritan had experienced enough storms in his own life, that just by looking at the wind damage, he knows a need is at hand. Authentic pastoral caregivers are experts in terms of analyzing wind damage. Just by looking at the way a tree has fallen, storm experts can tell the speed of the wind and the amount of internal damage that was inflicted by a particular storm. So can authentic pastoral caregivers.

I do propose that the Samaritan may have had some experience with being passed-over by others. The Samaritan perhaps knows all too well what it means when a person does not care whether you live or die. The Samaritans had lived in the shadows among the Jews. The Jews treatment of Samaritans was indeed less than noble, and the Jews' posture was one of superiority. The feeling of superiority of one group by another is never well received. The Jews, the chosen people of God, had somehow begun to see themselves as better than others, as opposed to as good as others. The truth, according to the book of Genesis 2, is humankind was formed from the dust of the earth. And there is just no way, one pile of dust can be better than another pile of dust.

"If you do it to the least of these...."

I am often frustrated by the classism that exists in the body of Christ today. At some churches, the poor and the destitute have been displaced. The poor and destitute have no way of financially supporting the Church; therefore, some churches find it hard to include them. Because they have no financial means, the poor and destitute are looked down upon condescendingly by some of the more blessed and highly favored Church members. They are viewed as not having done something right, therefore they are not ushered to the front pews of the church. There are no written rules concerning this; however, it is certainly spoken by the treatment and the body language of some so-called believers.

Who can administer authentic pastoral care? It is the person who has compassion in his or her heart. In this story, there is no other criterion or mandate. It merely suggests that those who have compassion in their hearts will be able to show it more readily than those who do not. Administering authentic pastoral care is not bound by race or religion. It transcends all lines of separation. Jesus speaks of the compassion of the Samaritan. The Samaritan sees the wounded man and has compassion for him! Jesus does not mention compassion when speaking about the priest and the Levite. The word *compassion* in Greek means "to be moved as to one's bowels." Hence to be moved with compassion, have compassion (for the bowels were thought to be the seat of love and pity) (Blue Letter Bible Online, 2010,). Webster defines *compassion* as: "sympathetic consciousness of others' distress together with a desire to alleviate it." (*Merriam-Webster Online*, 2010)

I recall being on duty one night at Grady Hospital in Atlanta. It was about 3:00 AM and a Muslim family was in crisis. This Muslim couple's newborn was having difficulties, and the doctors did not expect the child to make it through the night. A Muslim priest was summoned, but was delayed in coming. The longer we waited, the worse the newborn's condition seemed to get. The Muslim parents felt time was of the essence and asked if I would pray for their child. Without hesitation, I laid one hand upon the sick baby, and joined hands with my Muslim brother. He in turned grabbed his wife's hand, and we prayed in the Intensive Care Unit.

We crossed all boundaries and differences. This was not a time to review our differences in our expressions of God. It was time to look at our similarities. We all knew that we wanted healing for the baby according to God's will. How ever, that night we also became brothers and sisters. We were truly blessed because the Lord heard our prayer. The baby made it through the night and was able to go home a couple of days later.

In order to administer authentic pastoral care, we simply must possess the capacity for empathy toward those who are in need, no matter which religion or region of the world they live in. Authentic pastoral caregivers take courses, research online, and stay abreast of other religions and cultures.

We now have some insight into who needs authentic pastoral care and who administers it. In the next chapter, the story of the travelers on the Jericho Road will also provide some insight to "what is authentic pastoral care."

DISCUSSION QUESTIONS

1. Can pastors/caregivers take a day off? Why or why not?

2. Can pastors/caregivers help everybody? Why or why not?

3. How many of the pastor/priest/caregiver's own children's basketball/soccer/cheerleading practices should a pastor/priest/caregiver miss?

CASE STUDY II

Setting: A pastor comes home from the church late (again) one Thursday evening. The pastor has been counseling a couple and the session took a little longer than expected. However, it has been worth it because it appears the pastor has been instrumental in salvaging the marriage. The pastor opens the door and greets his/her spouse, but his/her spouse gives the silent treatment, never saying a word. The spouse continues to watch television with a bit of an angry stare on his/her face. The pastor says," Oh Lord, looks like it's going to be a long night…."

Pastor *(trying to sound cheerful)*: Hi honey!

Spouse: *(No response, more of a grunt)*

Pastor: Looks like I saved another marriage today. That couple was about to break-up. Their children have been in and out of trouble at school. The wife said she couldn't keep taking off of her job, and the husband said he could not keep taking off his job. I tell you, it was just a big 'ole mess….

Spouse: The school called today, Junior has been up to his old tricks again—cutting class. They want one of us to come to school tomorrow, but I've got a mandatory meeting at work…. *(Voice trailing off)*

Pastor: Well, you know I have got to meet the Chairman at the church and you know how he is; if I am not there, he sure will "let me have it."

Spouse: Why is it always about the Chairman? The Chairman does not pay any bills here, but it seems we are always paying him some money. I think you care more about Mr. Chairman than you care about your family. Remember that time a while back when you were sick, he did not even send your check that week, talking about if you don't preach, we don't pay....

Pastor: But you seem to keep forgetting, **I am the Pastor**!

Spouse: Yeah, you may be the pastor at the church, but your family is falling apart... (*Walks into bedroom, slams the door and locks it saying*) "Let's see if you can pastor that sofa tonight...."

CASE STUDY QUESTIONS

1. Should the pastor have called to say "I am going to be late, again?"

2. Is the pastor's marriage as important as the person he is counseling?

3. Why do you suppose the spouse is angry? Does the spouse have a reason to be angry?

4. Do you see any correlation between the marriage and the pastor's son acting out in school? If so, describe it.

5. What did the pastor do incorrectly?

_____
_____
_____
_____
_____
_____
_____
_____
_____

LESSONS FROM THE JERICHO ROAD

YOUR THOUGHTS

CHAPTER III
What is Authentic Pastoral Care?

We have talked about who needs authentic pastoral care, and we have discussed who can administer it. Now, we shall discuss what authentic pastoral care is and what it actually looks like. Perhaps we will find that it is more than using scriptures and prayers to attend to the wounds of the wounded.

> *He went to him and bandaged his wounds, having poured oil and wine on them. Then he put him on his own animal, brought him to an inn, and took care of him.* (Luke 10:34, NRSV)

Tending to the Wounded

Notice first, that the Samaritan goes to the wounded man. The Samaritan does not wait until the wounded man is able to come to him. The Samaritan makes the first move. Remember, the wounded man, in this case, is half-dead, inches from death. He does not wait until the wounded man can "get right or get himself together." The Samaritan is a man of action. As a child, most of us were taught that "actions speak louder than words." Sometimes there is no time or need for words, but one must be ready to work when work is available. Now is the acceptable time and today is the day.

Secondly, the Samaritan administers soothing oil and cleansing wine. The Samaritan begins to administer aid immediately. There are no questions concerning "How did you get here?", or "How did you let this happen?" The Samaritan pours oil and wine on the wounds. Oh! What compassion the Samaritan has by applying the soothing oil and the wine as a disinfectant at the same time. This is a lesson in administering authentic pastoral care. The wounded are soothed first with the oil as the wine is used to wash away the bacteria and cleanse the wound. Authentic pastoral care is gentle and effective at the same time. Here, the caregiver is not in a position to give a lecture, but he is here to bring comfort to another who is in an uncomfortable situation.

Notice not a word is spoken, but care is given. In this instance, action is required. There are many situations where words are not needed as much as the gentle ministry of presence.

Here is one minister's recollection of standing at the graveside of a loved-one; as he and other family members were saying their final goodbyes, he learned about the power of the ministry of presence. He was saying his final goodbyes to his loved-one, when an older gentleman came and laid his hand on his shoulder. The older gentleman didn't say anything. They both stood in complete silence. After a few moments of silence, the older gentlemen simply put his arm around the minister, embraced him with a hug and then walked away. He never spoke a word. A few years later, the minister ran across the old gentleman and asked him, "How did you know what not to say? My heart was broken into little pieces that day and yet it seemed that you understood more than the others?"

The older gentleman replied "Son, when my mother passed away, I realized that sometimes there are no words that can adequately express our sorrows in this world. But I also found out that Earth has no sorrow that heaven cannot heal." Pastors, ministers and lay persons can sometimes show their greatest effectiveness by simply standing with a grieving person in complete silence. This allows that person who is grieving to do proper diligence in their time of sorrow.

Thirdly, the Samaritan bandages up the wounds. We are left to our imagination as to what those bandages must have looked like. I would like to believe that the Samaritan takes one of his shirts out of his traveling bag and shreds it to make bandages. This suggests that the Samaritan has some experience in wound care. Whether through the Samaritan's own experience with his own wounds or some training in wound care, the results effective.

And finally, he stabilizes the wounded man out on the Jericho Road. He places the wounded man on his animal, takes him to the inn, and takes care of him. Notice the Samaritan does not leave the wounded man to complete his recovery on his own. He takes him to a safe location. A safe place where recovery can begin and all the steps of recovery can be completed.

I realize that I have spoken in general of what authentic pastoral care should look like in terms of oil, wine, wounds and bandages. However, here is a contemporary story of authentic pastoral care.

"When you stand up…."

This past summer I was jogging around Centennial Park in Atlanta, Georgia. It just happened to be a beautiful Sunday morning, and a church called "!mpact", pastored by Olu Brown, is having their worship service in the park. People are dressed casually in shorts and flip flops. So I joined in the crowd, thinking I would stop there and worship rather than run home, shower and make it to my church by the 11:00 AM service.

Sitting in front of me were two, school-age girls, probably 10 to 12 years old. And sitting next to me was a man and woman, who appeared to be in their early forties. While the preacher was preaching, one of the little girls, stood up to fold up her blanket. As she was standing, as little girls do, the woman next to me saw that the little girl's garments were not hanging appropriately. And before the little girl could unknowingly expose herself, the woman sitting next to me immediately stepped behind the little girl, and whispered in her ear, "When you stand up, pull your dress down!" And the woman pulled the little girl's dress down, avoiding a potentially embarrassing moment for the child. The little girl was startled at first, but fell back into the loving arms of this caring stranger. As the woman placed her arms around the little girl giving her a reassuring hug, I saw a smile come across the little girl's face.

This is an example of authentic pastoral care. The woman was not trying to make a name for herself by embarrassing the little girl. The woman did not scold the little girl or even ask, "Where is your mother?" She simply whispered in a very loving and caring way "When you stand up, make sure to check to be sure your dress is pulled all the way down!" And I noticed an immediate impact on the other little girl who was still on the ground. When the second little girl stood up, she checked to be sure her dress was pulled down. Only heaven knows the impact on these little girls because of the authentic pastoral care by this caring stranger.

This display of authentic pastoral care involved three distinct things: discretion, instruction and love. This kind of care is neither loud nor attention getting. There will be times when there is public notice of this greater good. There will be stories in the newspaper and the nightly news. However, in most cases, this is not the time to make a public display. It is a time of vulnerability for those to whom care is being given. The little girls were not exploited or humiliated in front of others. One of my favorite rules of thumb for leaders is to engage in "public praise, but private reprimand." One should never embarrass anyone into learning. Therefore, reprimanding should be done in a discreet manner, never in front of one's peers. And praise for a job well done, should be done as openly as possible and definitely in front of one's peers.

Secondly, proper instruction and feedback are received with less resistance if given in a caring way. Oftentimes, our children and loved-ones only hear the growl of instruction: "Don't do that!, Stand up straight!, Go wash your face, it's dirty! Stop! Shut up! Clean up this filthy room!" The unidentified woman's instruction was clear but kind: "When you stand up..." She even helped to smooth the back of the little girl's dress to enforce the gentle instruction.

And, finally this unidentified woman helps these girls by showing great love and compassion. It was very obvious to me that the woman understood the needs of the little girls at that time. Yes, there is a time for discipline, but somewhere in the unidentified woman's past, I would like to believe, she experienced this level of love from those around her. She knows how to speak in a loving way. She knows how to approach little girls in a loving way, and she knows how to embrace little girls in a loving way. I believe that 2 Corinthians 13 is correct:

> *Love is patient; love is kind; love is not envious or boastful or arrogant or rude. It does not insist on its own way; it is not irritable or resentful; it does not rejoice in wrongdoing, but rejoices in the truth.* [7]*It bears all things, believes all things, hopes all things, endures all things.* (NRSV)

DISCUSSION QUESTIONS

1. How did the Samaritan know how to administer this kind of pastoral care? Is it possible that he once had similar wounds or one of his loved-ones?

2. What do you think the Samaritan used for bandages?

3. Is it always wise to speak to children who are not yours?

4. Where do you think the unidentified women received her training?

CASE STUDY III

Setting: Frank, from the St. Mary's Chapel hospital visitation committee, is visiting a member in the hospital. He has heard rumors around the church that the member is seriously ill. However he has come, because the sick member sent word by his mother that he wanted a visit from the pastor.
(Frank enters the room with his hands in his pockets)

Frank: How are you doing son?

Joel: Not too bad, considering the circumstances. Where is the pastor?

Frank: He could not come today, but your mother told me that you asked to see the pastor. So I came in his place. She said you had a very pressing question.

Joel: I do Sir... I have a question and I was hoping the pastor could answer it for me.

Frank: *(Moves from the door to the foot of the bed, with his hands still in his pockets)* Well son, I will try.

Joel: Is my sickness because of my sins? Is God punishing me?

Frank: I hope that is not the case...because if sickness is punishment from God, then we all would be sick. None of us have lived the perfect life. As a matter of fact, only one man ever did, and they hung him on a cross. No one chooses a certain illness. No one goes around saying I want to have cancer, diabetes, hypertension, or any other disease... seems to me the illnesses do the picking and we do the suffering. However, to answer your question, the reason that you are sick and the reason that you have your kind of sickness, I don't really know... seems everybody has a cross to bear....

Joel: Well thank you sir for coming...I feel a little better now because it was really worrying me....

Frank: *(Moves to head of the bed, lays hands on Joel's head and whispers a powerful prayer... so powerful that tears fall from Joel's eyes....)*

CASE STUDY QUESTIONS

1. Why do you feel Frank keeps his hands in his pockets during the first part of the visit?

2. Why do you think Joel feels the way he does about his sickness?

3. Do you think Frank gives Joel a fair answer? Is Frank or the Pastor supposed to have the correct answer?

4. Is sickness a sign of a big sinner? Consider the Bible story of the man born blind: Who sinned, the blind man or his parents?

_____
_____
_____
_____
_____
_____
_____
_____
_____
_____

LESSONS FROM THE JERICHO ROAD

YOUR THOUGHTS

CHAPTER IV
What Happens After Authentic Pastoral Care?

Firstly, we examined who needs authentic pastoral care. Secondly, we discussed who can administer it. Thirdly, we considered what authentic pastoral care is and what it actually looks likes, then and now. In this chapter, we will discuss what happens after authentic pastoral care has been administered.

> *The next day he took out two denarii, gave them to the innkeeper, and said, 'Take care of him; and when I come back, I will repay you whatever more you spend.'* (Luke 10:35, NRSV)

In verse 35, the story moves to the final step in the authentic pastoral care process. It shows how others are intrinsically involved and how their help is needed. On the next day, the Samaritan gives two denarii to the innkeeper. One denarius is equal to a day's wages; therefore the Samaritan gives the innkeeper two days of wages to take care of this wounded stranger. (Blue Letter Bible, 1996)

He said, "Take care of him, and when I come back, I will repay you whatever more you spend." The Samaritan has been very responsive to the wounded man. He rescued the wounded man, brought him to a place of safety, and stayed with him until he was stabilized. But now the Samaritan is remembering that he must continue his own journey. He realizes he cannot stay with the wounded man forever, so he turns the responsibility over to the innkeeper.

As authentic pastoral caregivers, it is imperative that we understand that we have limitations. In this case, the Samaritan helps stabilize the wounded man and moves him to a place of safety. We, however, must ensure that as pastors, ministers, and caregivers, we do not over-burden ourselves. In rescuing others, there are other agencies set up to aid people who are in crisis. As authentic pastoral caregivers, we can provide even greater care by knowing where those agencies are located, what services they provide, and who they can assist. When caring for others begins to hurt us, we've taken it too far.

One pastor recalled how he tried to help someone battle drug addiction and almost lost his entire ministry. The pastor said he soon realized that he was not an addiction counselor and that he was not equipped to help a person caught up in the world of drug addiction. The addicted person needs a structured environment not often found in the local church setting. Yes, the Church can provide love, healing, and prayer, but it cannot always provide the professional structured care found in other agencies. The Samaritan is wise enough to understand that at this point in his story, "I need to put this individual in the hands of the innkeeper, someone who is familiar with the art of hospitality," so that I may continue my own journey.

An important part of authentic pastoral care understands that the person giving care, will, from time to time need to take care of their own needs. That is not to say that the person providing authentic pastoral care will always put their needs before others. However, the person providing care should remember to take time to care for their own needs as well, such as taking a vacation, going to a movie, attending a ball game, enjoying a concert, or spending quality time with family and spouse. One very prominent successful pastor in the city of Atlanta, GA, among the innumerable responsibilities that fall upon him, still finds time to go bowling.

As we revisit the life of Jesus, we see that this was a daily pattern of Jesus. In the morning and evenings, Jesus had private time. Jesus would go to the mountains or remote places to get away from the crowds. Jesus would always manage to find quiet time to spend part of his day in communion with his Father. Yes, we must work while it is day, which suggests that work is done during the day, but night is a time of rest, sleep, and restoration. It appears seemingly impossible for any one individual to do what Jesus did, and at the pace Jesus did it. He literally changed a world in three and half years.

The Responsibility of the Innkeeper

At first, I was a little disturbed with this idea of the Samaritan creating work for the innkeeper. I presume that the innkeeper probably already has enough to do. The innkeeper has other guests and now the innkeeper is burdened with the responsibility of caring for someone who may need constant around-the-clock attention. Innkeepers in those days prepared breakfast, lunch and dinner. They made the beds, washed the laundry, cleaned the bathrooms, swept the floors and fed the animals. Their staff was often limited to the members of their family.

However, as I now understand the innkeeper, his job is to take care of the guests. As a matter of fact, the innkeeper dedicates himself to taking care of guests. The innkeeper has specialized training in providing care to guests. No wonder the Samaritan says, "Take care of him! And when I come back, I will repay you whatever more you spend." This specialized training includes knowing what care and delivery of care the wounded man will need in order to find full restoration. The wounded man is left in very capable hands.

Authentic Pastoral Care to Hospitals and Homes

Authentic caregivers will need to be sensitive to the time frames and procedures when visiting or ministering to those in need. This is especially true for those making visits to hospitals, and homes of those in need. When you enter the hospital keep the following in mind:

1. Enter the patient's room as quietly as possible. There are other patients on the floor or in the same room that need their quiet time.

2. Check at the nurse's station to determine if this is a good time. The patient may be bathing, taking medicine, or receiving treatment. Their needs change from moment to moment.

3. Do not sit on the bed or rearrange the room. Tables and chairs are in place so the patient can reach the table with ease.

4. Do not open blinds and windows unless asked to do so by the patient; their eyes may be sensitive to the light.

5. Please read any scripture quietly and pray accordingly. The hospital may not necessarily be the place for a "revival type prayer."

6. Do not stay long. I repeat, do not stay long. Patients are resting and recuperating. Patients are lying flat on their backs, dressed in hospital robes. They are not necessarily up for candid conversation or entertaining guests. A recommended visit time is 15-20 minutes.

The same protocol and procedures apply to home visits. Please call before arriving, even though your appointment may have been scheduled ahead of time. A homebound person's needs may change by the hour. The effects of different medicines may cause a change in the way the person may feel. Again, the rule of thumb is not to stay long; however, home visits tend to last a few moments longer. Bear in mind the needs of the person you are visiting. Some people who do not have a lot of family and those that have been homebound for a period of time may enjoy a few extra minutes of your time (minutes, not hours).

Please keep the visit as pleasant and as positive as possible. This is not a good time to talk about your personal problems or personal grievances with the church or other members. In terms of reading the scriptures, a few verses are appropriate. The prayers should be soothing and passionate. Please be reminded that God is not hard of hearing, and neither are others that may be present. Long, loud prayers may interfere with the patient taking medicines on time and their comfort. The length of visit rule also applies here regarding the potential for the medical needs of the person you are visiting changing from moment to moment. If you stay too long, it might necessitate you being asked to leave, causing embarrassment for both the patient and you as the caregiver.

Prayer for healing should be according to "God's will" as opposed to "right now." I do believe that some individuals have the gift of healing, and the gift of laying on of hands and those miracles do occur. However, those that have the gift still realize that healing can only come through God and in God's own time. God may not come when we call upon Him, but assuredly God is always on-time. God moves in mysterious ways to ensure that God gets the glory, and not us.

And finally, be sensitive to the person or persons being visited. Dr. Carolyn L. McCrary, Professor of Pastoral Counseling at the Interdenominational Theological Center of Atlanta, Georgia, often recounts the time she visited a parishioner who was homebound. The parishioner asked her whether she knew a certain song. And, of course, she knew the song. He asked her to sing just one verse. Now this was before a prayer was spoken or a scripture was read. Dr. McCrary says she ministered more to the man by song than by scripture because that was what he needed at the time.

Sometimes the visit will be spontaneous and the person being visited will be full of conversation. Yet at other times, the visit may require the best of your listening skills. Being quiet and still is different than doing nothing at all. It requires your undivided attention and sensitive spiritual discernment of the moment at hand. This discernment may reveal that other needs are present such as the need for a housekeeper or social worker. Someone may need to come by and cut the grass or ensure the trash is taken out. Authentic pastoral care allows us to not only see with our eyes, but see with our hearts and souls as well.

Bereavement

The time of bereavement is a very sensitive time. Even if it is expected, one still cannot adequately prepare for death. It has such finality, and there is no one to argue the point that the loved-one may have needed to stay a little while longer. At the time of death, many are longing for one more word or perhaps even one more touch. Death has a distinguishable pain.

Depending on the relationship of the lost loved one and

those left behind, the pain can be quite unbearable. Many believe that the loss should be gotten over quickly and the living should move on with their lives. That may be true for some; but again, depending on the relationship, the death of a loved-one can be both devastating and debilitating. Psychologists report that, depending on the closeness of the relationship, grief recovery takes one to three years.

According to the scriptures, when Jesus lost his friend, "he wept." (KJV) He cried tears of sorrow. And these are not the little tears that form in the corner of the eye and can be wiped away with a tissue. These are those big crocodile tears that flood over our cheeks, down our faces, and lap under our chins. It is as though the floodgates have opened and no one can close them. Weeping is different from crying. Death can be described as a house of pain, and we are forced to spend many nights there. The pain is often enough to cause one to almost lose consciousness. The grief recovery process is not the same for every individual. Here are the steps of the grieving process, not every person will pass through the phases necessarily in this order:

- **Shock** – Person is speechless after receiving news of the loss of loved-one. Expresses feelings of numbness or foggy-thinking.

- **Denial** – Person refuses to believe it's true that their loved-one has passed on. They say things like, "I can't believe John's gone."

- **Anger** – Person is angry, sometimes even with God, for the loss of their loved-one. They might blame a doctor, hospital or relatives.

- **Bargaining** – Person tries to strike a deal, will do whatever it takes if their loved-one is returned. They may say things like, "I will go to church every Sunday," or "I will give up drinking, smoking, etc. ...."

- **Acceptance.** Person finally accepts the fact that their loved-one has passed on. They are able to speak of their loved-one without sobbing and have accepted that the loved one is gone. He or she is getting use to life without the deceased person.

Again, persons may or may not go through the stages as listed, but they will generally pass through all the stages. Individuals can also go through a stage and return to it again. Often I have seen members cry on Mother's Day, or Father's Day, and I would wonder why they are still crying. Their loved-one passed years ago. However, now that my mother and father have passed away, I understand fully why we still find ourselves crying. Death is a very painful situation. When undergoing medical procedures one can opt for pain killers such as morphine drips and epidurals.Unfortunately, when a loved-one dies, there are no morphine drips or epidurals. But, we have this hope that our forefathers left us. They remind us that "Earth has no sorrow, which heaven cannot heal!" As a caregiver, you'll want to be prepared. Please remember:

- **The time of death is not the time to train members about protocol.**

The church should prepare members for death before the time comes. Workshops and checklists should be a part of the new members' packet as well as continuing members' training.

- **Call the family as soon as possible after hearing of a death.**

If by chance, word is received that a loss has occurred, please do not hesitate to call family and confirm. Remember the family is in a state of shock or denial and may not think to call you in a timely manner. Try to limit funeral arrangements with just one person. Talking with too many family members about funeral arrangements can be confusing, causing times and dates to get lost in translation.

- **Call the funeral home as soon as possible.**

To avoid overbooking your schedule, please call the funeral home, so that you and the funeral director are aware of the dates available. There are instances when the funeral is planned and then the pastor is called. This may be a conflict in terms that there may be a wedding scheduled at the church on the same day and time the funeral is now being planned.

- **Call ahead to let the family know when you are coming.**

A rule of thumb is to always call to confirm the scheduled visit. There may be some very heated discussions going on, and the family may need you to come at another time. Also, on the day of the funeral, please call the family and confirm your availability to them. Assure the family that you will be with them as they walk through the valley and the shadow of death.

- **Be prepared.**

The day of the funeral is usually a long one. Try to get as much rest as possible. Funerals are also emotional and spiritually demanding for two reasons. Firstly, the family is depending on the pastor or minister for an unusual amount of support. Secondly, there are new and different family members and friends that are also depending on the pastor or minister for support. The pastor or minister must be careful not to deplete her or his own spiritual and emotional resources.

Marriage

Each church will have its own theology about marriage. The important thing to remember is that marriage counseling should be strongly advised. Also, it should be carried out by someone who has premarital training and/or some experience in the subject matter. It would be understandable if a couple decided to be counseled by a minister that is married as opposed to a minister who has never been married. If single, maintain a list of married ministers that you can recommend. Remember to discuss the arrangement with the recommended minister beforehand.

Counseling

Discretion is priority number one! Pastors and caregivers must take extreme caution when information is revealed to them. Most, if not all, conversations should not be shared. The exception is when a person's life is in danger. That includes the person being counseled as well as the person who may be harmed by the person being counseled. Please be abreast of local laws as well as state and federal laws regarding counseling and confidentiality. I do caution pastors and caregiver to rely on other certified counselors. In particularly, I remind pastors that it is difficult to construct sermons that do not relate to someone in the congregation as counseling continues. If a pastor preaches about something, that a parishioner has not shared with the pastor, then the parishioner will see this as divine intervention. However, when a pastor preaches about something that a parishioner has revealed to that pastor, the parishioner may assume that the pastor is sharing the parishioner's information. In essence, if an outside source is used for counseling, then the parishioner will remain confident their information is not being shared.

In terms of self care, both the pastor and caregiver should have resources for counseling for themselves. In most cases, help is often sought too late, after burnout occurs, or after some self-inflicted damage is done. Counseling should be in place before one reaches this point. This counseling can be very professional or casual in nature, just make sure the pastor or caregiver can vent. Also, this assistance would be best administered by outside sources as opposed to along denominational lines or corporate plans. This will give the pastor or caregiver a greater sense of confidentiality and they may be willing to reveal more.

DISCUSSION QUESTIONS

1. Was the Samaritan obligated to offer extend care to the robbed man?

2. Did the Samaritan create more work for the innkeeper?

3. Can you identify places in your community that wounded people can be taken?

4. What could be some embarrassing moments for patients while being visited?

CASE STUDY IV

Setting: Joe is coming home from work. As he steps in the door, his wife Sue hugs him, kisses him swiftly on the cheek, and hurries out of the door.

Sue: Dinner is in the oven, and please help Sarah, with her homework. Her teacher says that in order for her to pass to the fifth grade, she is going to have to pass math.

Joe: And where are you going?

Sue: They just called, the trustees want me to come to the church tonight for the trustee meeting. We are going look at the Blueprints for the new building.

Joe: *(Bitterly)* Why did "they" not do this last night while "you" were at bible study? Sure is a lot going on at church lately. What happened when you went to church on Monday and Tuesday? And you have a meeting on Saturday at the church, can it wait till then? And when did you become a trustee?

Sue: The blueprints were not ready then.

Joe: Oh, but they are ready now?

Sue: Oh, Joe, I am just trying to help. Like Pastor says "We are a growing church and he needs everyone to help out." And no, I am not a trustee.

Joe: Seems to me, you are doing all the helping, and everybody else is sitting on their hands….

Sue: *(argumentatively)* Yes, they are really depending on me. And they know that I know a lot about the church, because I have been there since the beginning. No one knows as much about the church as I do! They need me! And I am not going to let them change our church into the latest fad! I will talk to you, when I get back!

CASE STUDY QUESTIONS

1. How many days does Sue spend at church?

2. The church is growing, but is she the only one that can help the pastor?

3. Is it good for her to be at the church that much? After all, the church is growing.

4. Does Jim have a right to be upset?

5. Does the church need Sue or does Sue need the church?

_____
_____
_____
_____
_____
_____
_____
_____

LESSONS FROM THE JERICHO ROAD

YOUR THOUGHTS

CHAPTER V
"What then shall we say to these things…?"

> *"Which of these three, do you think, was a neighbor to the man who fell into the hands of the robbers?" He said, "The one who showed him mercy." Jesus said to him, "Go and do likewise."* (Luke 10:37, NRSV)

As the story ends, it appears that the lawyer has the right answer, but the wrong question. The lawyer's question is, "Who is my neighbor?" The question that Jesus is suggesting that the lawyer ask is, "Not who is my neighbor, but who was a neighbor to the man?" Jesus asked "Which of these three do you think is a neighbor to the man who fell into the hands of robbers?" The lawyer is able to draw a very accurate conclusion. He says, "The one who showed mercy!" Jesus then says to him "You go and do likewise."

Authentic pastoral care suggests that we, too, must go and do likewise. Part of our divine assignment is to tend to the needs of those who are unable to help themselves.

Firstly, we now have an understanding of who needs authentic pastoral care: Those that are put in a position where they cannot help themselves. Secondly, we now have an understanding of just who is able to administer authentic pastoral care: The Samaritan saw the wounded man and had compassion on him. Thirdly, we have a very vivid understanding of what authentic pastoral care looks like: The Samaritan tended to the wounded man and stabilized his situation. And finally, we have a working knowledge of what should happen after authentic pastoral care is administered: The Samaritan took the wounded man to a safe and secure location. He provided structured after care for the wounded man. More importantly, the Samaritan can now continue his journey.

Hopefully, we understand that as a pastor, minister or caregiver, you do not have to do it all by yourself. There are agencies that work hand in hand with churches and are available to provide a structured environment for healing and wholeness.

Authentic Pastoral Care is Person-Driven

After our study here, we can conclude:

• Not every wounded person's need is the same.

• We do not always know what people need.

• There is no blueprint for authentic pastoral care.
    • Some prefer scripture reading
    • Some prefer singing
    • Some prefer sermons
    • Some need dishes washed/grass cut/meals cooked

•Some have other needs that require specialized training. For example:
    • Premature birth/post birth counseling
    • Marital/domestic/relationship counseling
    • Children at home/children away from home counseling
    • Substance abuse and sexual abuse counseling

Triangle of Pastoral Care

Moreover, authentic pastoral care can further be explained by using what is called the "Triangle of Pastoral Care." Notice the triangle is a continuum. All three agencies are interdependent upon each other.

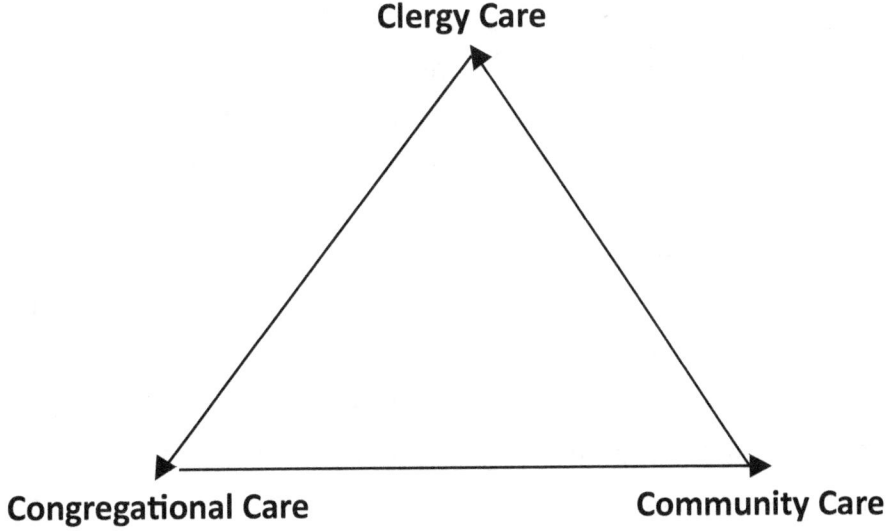

Clergy Care

Clergy Care is extremely vital. One of the most important things that clergy and caregivers can do is learn how to live a balanced life. That means balancing the needs of ministry and their own personal needs: love, family, shelter, and safety. If a person's life is splintered and broken into pieces, it is difficult to care for others. Caregivers and ministers that are weary and worn thin are more likely to make careless choices and mistakes. As I understand it, Jesus' yoke is easy and His burden is light. An ancient Chinese proverb says "Less is more." Could we as ministers and caregivers be doing too much?

Often pastors, ministers and caregivers have been trained proficiently in the care of others. However, little training is done in terms of how one should take care of one's self. One of the main components of authentic pastoral care is training in self-care. The question has been asked, "Where does the shepherd go, when the shepherd needs a shepherd?" What do pastors and caregivers do, when the weight of the world is on their shoulder?

Self-care begins with doing some of the simple things in life. Perhaps taking in a movie, going to lunch with friends, riding a bike, taking a walk, playing golf, going to a sports game, going shopping and the list goes on. Dr. Lynderia Cheevers, Education Specialist for the CDC of Atlanta, suggests "it is imperative for us to take time to do those things that make deposits into our souls, rather than withdrawals." We have to cultivate resources that feed our soul even in a church setting.

One of the things I like to do when visiting another church is to sit in the pews rather than sit on the dais with the pastors and ministers. Often, when I get a chance to visit churches like Antioch North, located in Atlanta, GA, my needs are so great, that I literally find myself crawling in the back door. My capacity to give is completely depleted and I am in need of spiritual refreshment. Then the pastor Reverend Dr. Cameron Alexander stands in the pulpit and in his own wonderful style, ministers in such a way that I feel that he is speaking directly to me. My soul is fed, my cup runs over and my storage tank is no longer empty.

Congregational Care

If the clergy and caregivers are whole, then they can be more effective in ministering to the needs of the congregation and the community. The congregational needs can be more readily assessed and ministered to when those providing the help are of optimum health. Those who receive care at the hands of whole caregivers tend to reach recovery, restoration, and transformation more quickly. The restored congregation can then tend to their own needs without overwhelming the clergy and caregivers. This means less strain and stress for the clergy and caregivers.

Community Care

Healthy clergy and caregivers produce healthy congregations and care recipients. Therefore healthy congregations and care recipients are more readily prepared to access and take of the needs of the community. This will result in stronger and better communities that are able to resolve their own issues. Strong communities are able to articulate and bring into existence their dreams and desires. The village is able to build and strengthen the villagers by managing and policing its own ideals concerning community trust. Strong communities are then, in effect, more able to strengthen the congregations and the clergy by providing grants and other financial support to the ministries and programs of a healthy congregation.

CONCLUSION

We have discovered that authentic pastoral care can take many forms. As we have read from referenced biblical accounts, a calling is not always to a pulpit ministry, but it is multifaceted and covers other vocations besides the priesthood. It comes in the form of building boats, feeding multitudes, giving sight to the blind, setting captives free, or simply, rebuilding walls. It also translates into shelters, rehabilitation centers, temporary and permanent housing, job training, temporary and permanent jobs, computer literacy, education for traditional and non-traditional students, and amateur and pro athletes. Authentic pastoral care is large, corporate, and global; and at the same time, it may be simply buying a cup of coffee for a stranger. It is ministry to all and in every imaginable context.

BIBLIOGRAPHY/REFERENCES

Blue Letter Bible. 1996-2010. 13 Jun 2010. http://www.blueletterbible.org

"Compassion Fatigue - Because You Care". St. Petersburg Bar Association Magazine. http://www.transitionsandyou.com/Compassion_Fatigue.pdf. Retrieved 2010-12.

http://aapc.org/content/what-pastoral-counseling July 26, 2010
©2005-2009 American Association of Pastoral Counselors

Merriam-Webster Online Dictionary. Retrieved 13 June 2010, http://www.merriam-webster.com

Wiersbe, Warren, W. *The Bible Exposition Commentary: New Testament Vol 1*. Colorado Springs, 2001

Wimberly, Edward P., *African American Pastoral Care*. Nashville: Abingdon Press, 1991

RECOMMENDED READINGS

Cahill, Lisa Sowle. *Families: A Christian Social Perspective.* Minneapolis, MN: Fortress Press, 2000.

Chimmarusti, Rocco A. and Jay Lappin. "Beginning Family Therapy." *Family Therapy Collections,* no. 14 (1985).

Dash, Michael I.N., Jonathan Jackson, and Stephen C. Rasor. *Hidden Wholeness: An African American Spirituality for Individuals and Communities.* Cleveland, OH: United Church Press, 1997.

Erickson, E. H. *Childhood and Society.* New York: Norton, 1950. Miller, Donald Eugene. Congregations: *Their Power to Form and Transform.* Atlanta, GA: John Knox Press, 1988.

Robertson, Anita. *Learning While Leading: Increasing Your Effectiveness In Ministry.* New York, NY: The Alban Institute, 2000.

Schleiermacher, Friedrich D. E. *Absolute Dependence.* 1821: English translation of 2nd ed. (accessed April 18, 2003) available from http://people.bu.edu/wwildman/WeirdWildWeb/courses/mwt/ dictionary/methemes; Internet.

Smith, Alanzo H., and June Smith. "Parishioner Attitudes Toward the Divorced/Separated: Awareness Seminars as Counseling Interventions." In Counseling & Values, no. 45 (October 2000).

Vassiliou, George A. "Analogic Communications as a Means of Joining the Family System in Therapy." *International Journal of Family Psychiatry,* no. 4 (2003).